Communities

HARCOURT BRACE SOCIAL STUDIES

D1227059

ACTIVITY BOOK

Teacher's Edition

HARCOURT BRACE & COMPANY

Orlando Atlanta Austin Boston San Francisco Chicago Dallas

New York Toronto London

Visit The Learning Site at http://www.hbschool.com

The activities in this book reinforce or extend social studies concepts and skills in **COMMUNITIES.** There is one activity for each content lesson, skill, or Write-On Chart lesson. Reproductions of the activity pages appear with answers in the Teacher's Edition.

CONTENTS

Write-On Charts

CONTENTS

WHERE
on
EARTH?

Show Location

**DIRECTIONS: Follow the instructions to fill out each
of the address labels below.**

Fill out this label to tell where your school is located.

School Name _____

City or Town _____

State _____

Country United States _____

Continent North America _____

Hemispheres Northern/Western _____

Fill out this label to tell where you were born.

City or Town _____

State _____

Country _____

Continent _____

Hemispheres _____

HOW TO READ A MAP

 Apply Map and Globe Skills

DIRECTIONS: Study the map of Arizona. Use what you have learned about reading maps to complete the activities below.

1. Circle the title of the map.

2. Add the missing direction letters to the compass rose.

3. Place an **X** on the name of the state that is east of Arizona.

4. In the map key, what does the symbol ▓ show?

   National parks
   _____

5. Use the distance scale to measure how many miles it is between Kingman and Prescott. Write that distance here. about 100 miles
   _____

6. Now use the distance scale to see how many miles it is from Lake Havasu City to Grand Canyon National Park. Write that distance here. about 150 miles

MAKING LAWS

Imagine that your class is a town like Roxaboxen. You have been chosen to help make the laws for your town.

Understand Rules and Laws

DIRECTIONS: Think of two laws that will help make your imaginary town safe. Write your laws on the lines below. Give one reason why each law is needed. Give two possible consequences of breaking each law.

Law Number 1

Direct students to create practical laws.

_____

Reason for the Law

Look for an understanding of the need for laws.

_____

_____

Consequences of
Breaking the Law

1. Help students connect actions with consequences.

2. _____

Law Number 2

_____

_____

Reason for the Law

_____

_____

Consequences of
Breaking the Law

1. _____

2. _____

NAME _____ DATE _____

HOW TO ACT AS A RESPONSIBLE CITIZEN

Participation Skills

DIRECTIONS: Each day of the chart below lists a way to be a responsible citizen. In each space, write a sentence that tells how you can do the activity at home, at school, or in your neighborhood.

Look for practical applications of the suggestions to the students' lives.

MONDAY	TUESDAY
Clean up litter.	Follow traffic safety laws.

WEDNESDAY	THURSDAY
Learn about current events.	Save energy.

FRIDAY	SATURDAY
Share with people who need help.	Reuse and recycle materials.

Use after reading Unit 1, Skill Lesson, page 52.

VOLUNTEERS NEEDED!

Apply Matching Skills

DIRECTIONS: The people in Column A want to be volunteers. The signs in Column B show places that need volunteers. Draw a line from each volunteer in Column A to the sign with the matching need in Column B.

COLUMN A	COLUMN B

1. Kyle likes to cook.

2. Hayley writes books for children.

3. Mark knows how to build walls.

VOLUNTEERS NEEDED
TO READ STORIES
TO CHILDREN
AT THE LIBRARY!

VOLUNTEERS NEEDED
TO REBUILD HOUSES
DAMAGED BY THE STORM!

VOLUNTEERS NEEDED
TO MAKE AND DELIVER
HOT MEALS TO
PEOPLE!

NAME _____ DATE _____

A YUMA ALBUM

Identify Historical Times in Pictures

DIRECTIONS: Each picture below shows a scene from a different time in the history of Yuma. The times are listed for you in the box. Look at the pictures. Then write the correct time under each picture.

TIMES IN YUMA HISTORY

- Quechan times
- Spanish missionary times
- Anglo and Chinese settler times
- Yuma today

1. Spanish missionary times

2. Yuma today

3. Quechan times

4. Anglo and Chinese settler times

6 ACTIVITY BOOK

Use after reading Unit 1, Lesson 4, pages 56–60.

HOW TO READ A TIME LINE

Apply Chart and Graph Skills

DIRECTIONS: The time line below shows some important events in the history of Arizona. It covers 100 years, from 1860 to 1960. Use the information on the time line to help you answer the questions that follow.

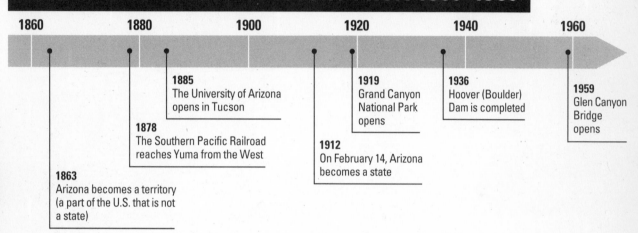

TIME LINE OF ARIZONA HISTORY FROM 1860–1960

1860   1880   1900   1920   1940   1960

1885
The University of Arizona opens in Tucson

1878
The Southern Pacific Railroad reaches Yuma from the West

1863
Arizona becomes a territory (a part of the U.S. that is not a state)

1919
Grand Canyon National Park opens

1912
On February 14, Arizona becomes a state

1936
Hoover (Boulder) Dam is completed

1959
Glen Canyon Bridge opens

1. Which is older, Glen Canyon Bridge or Hoover Dam?

Hoover Dam (completed in 1936)

2. Was Arizona first a territory or a state? Arizona was first a territory (created in 1863).

3. In what year did the University of Arizona open? 1885

4. Which national park opened in 1919? Grand Canyon National Park

5. Why do you think Arizona was nicknamed the Valentine State?

Arizona became a state on Valentine's Day (February 14) in 1912.

(Continued)

DIRECTIONS: The time line below shows one week. Think of two things that happened to you last week. Make entries for these two things on the time line. Illustrate your entries with small drawings.

TIME LINE FOR ONE WEEK

Sunday	Monday	Tuesday	Wednesday	Thursday	Friday	Saturday

CULTURE CROSSWORD

Solve a Word Puzzle

DIRECTIONS: Use the clues on the next page to solve the crossword puzzle.

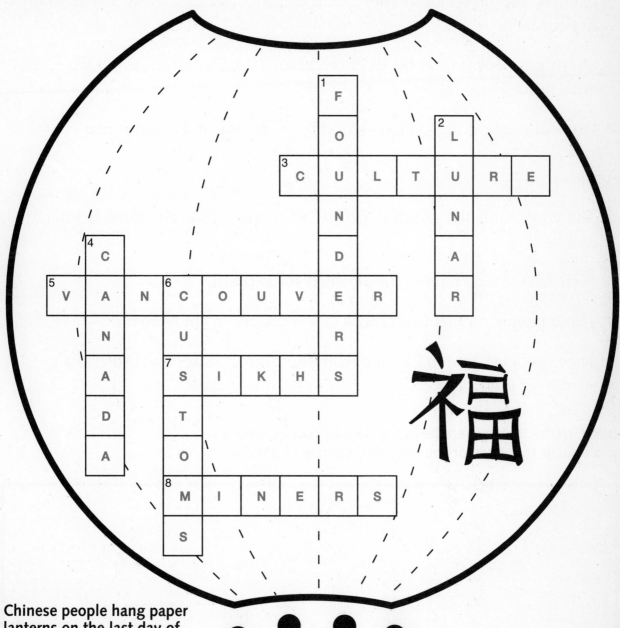

Crossword answers:

1. Down: FOUNDER
2. Down: LUNAR
3. Across: CULTURE
4. Down: CANADA
5. Across: VANCOUVER
6. Down: CUSTOMS
7. Across: SIKHS
8. Across: MINERS

Chinese people hang paper lanterns on the last day of the New Year festival. The design on this lantern is a Chinese character, or picture-word, that means "good fortune."

(Continued)

CLUES

Down

1. The people who start a community.

2. Chinese people celebrate the _____ New Year, usually in February.

4. On July 1, people in Vancouver celebrate _____ Day with fireworks.

6. Ways of doing things, often shared by members of a community.

Across

3. The way of life of a group of people who often share the same language and beliefs.

5. A city in Canada named for a British sea captain.

7. These people moved from India to Vancouver to cut timber.

8. These people came to Canada from the United States and Australia to search for gold.

DIRECTIONS: In the space below, draw a picture or write a short poem about one of your favorite customs or holidays.

What Is a Community?

Connect Main Ideas

DIRECTIONS: Use this graphic organizer to show that you understand how the unit's main ideas are connected. Complete this graphic organizer by writing one detail about each community. The details should tell more about each lesson's main idea.

Lesson 1
A community has a location on Earth.

1. Roxaboxen: corner of 2nd Avenue and 8th Street

2. Yuma: In Arizona

Lesson 5
A community is made up of different groups of people who live and work together.

1. Roxaboxen: girls formed a group

2. Yuma: many different people live in Yuma

Lesson 2
Citizens in a community form governments and work together to solve problems.

1. Roxaboxen: police officer Jamie

2. Yuma: police officer

What Is a Community?

Lesson 4
A community changes over time.

1. Roxaboxen: children left the community

2. Yuma: grew into a modern city

Lesson 3
People in a community use resources to meet their needs.

1. Roxaboxen: stones to make streets

2. Yuma: wood to build houses

PLACE NAMES

Classify Physical Features

DIRECTIONS: Draw a line from the name in the left column to the correct type of physical feature in the right column.

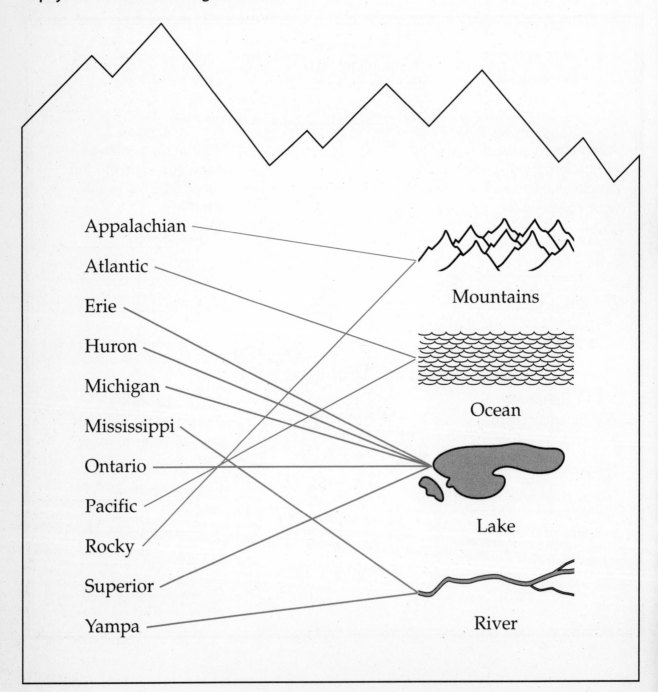

Appalachian

Atlantic

Erie

Huron

Michigan

Mississippi

Ontario

Pacific

Rocky

Superior

Yampa

Mountains

Ocean

Lake

River

Use after reading Unit 2, Lesson 1, pages 88–95.

NAME _____ DATE _____

HOW TO READ A LANDFORM MAP

Apply Map and Globe Skills

DIRECTIONS: Study this landform map of Ohio. Then use what you have learned about reading landform maps to answer the questions on the next page.

OHIO LANDFORMS

MICHIGAN

Lake Erie

PENNSYLVANIA

Toledo

LAKE PLAINS

Cleveland

Aurora

Akron   Youngstown

N
W   E
S

INDIANA

INTERIOR PLAINS

OHIO

ALLEGHENY PLATEAU

Columbus

Dayton

Cincinnati

Ohio River

0   25   50 Miles
0   25   50 Kilometers

Plateau
Plain
Hills

KENTUCKY

WEST VIRGINIA

(Continued)

NAME _____ DATE _____

1. Find the map key. What landform is shown with slanted lines?

plain
_____

2. What landform is shown with this symbol: [⌒⌒] ?

hills
_____

3. There are two plains areas located in Ohio. What are they called?

Lake Plains, Interior Plains
_____

_____

4. On what landform is Aurora located? plateau _____

_____

5. Which Ohio city is on higher ground, Akron or Cincinnati?

Akron
_____

6. Which two cities are located on the Lake Plains?

Toledo, Cleveland
_____

7. Which three cities are located on the Interior Plains?

Columbus, Dayton, Cincinnati
_____

8. The Lake Plains are next to which body of water?

Lake Erie
_____

9. On this map, which Ohio city is farthest east on the Allegheny Plateau?

Youngstown
_____

10. Ohio is not located on very high ground. How can you tell that from this

map? There are no mountains shown on the landform map of Ohio.
_____

_____

CITIES ON THE WATER

ATLANTIC OCEAN
Boston, Massachusetts
Miami, Florida
New York, New York

PACIFIC OCEAN
Portland, Oregon
San Diego, California
Seattle, Washington

GULF OF MEXICO
Galveston, Texas
Mobile, Alabama
Tampa, Florida

GREAT LAKES
Buffalo, New York
Chicago, Illinois
Milwaukee, Wisconsin

MISSISSIPPI RIVER
Baton Rouge, Louisiana
Dubuque, Iowa
St. Paul, Minnesota

MISSOURI RIVER
Great Falls, Montana
Kansas City, Kansas
Omaha, Nebraska

The chart at left shows major bodies of water and some U.S. cities located on them.

Use Information from a Chart

DIRECTIONS: Use the information in the chart to tell whether each sentence below is true or false. If it is true, write a T on the line. If it is false, write an F on the line and explain why it is false on a separate sheet of paper.

__T__ **1.** Portland, Oregon, is located near the Pacific Ocean.

__F__ **2.** San Diego, California, and Dubuque, Iowa, are located on the same river. San Diego is on the Pacific Ocean; Dubuque is on the Mississippi River.

__F__ **3.** Chicago, Illinois, is located on the Missouri River. It is on one of the Great Lakes.

__T__ **4.** Galveston, Texas, is located on the Gulf of Mexico.

__F__ **5.** Buffalo, New York, is not located near a Great Lake. It is on one of the Great Lakes.

__F__ **6.** Boston, Massachusetts, and Miami, Florida, are located on the Pacific Ocean. Both are on the Atlantic Ocean.

__T__ **7.** You could travel from Baton Rouge, Louisiana, to St. Paul, Minnesota, on the same body of water.

HOW TO READ A TABLE

Apply Chart and Graph Skills

DIRECTIONS: Use the table below to answer the questions that follow.

FIVE MOST POPULATED STATES IN THE UNITED STATES	
STATE	**POPULATION**
California	29,760,021
New York	17,990,455
Texas	16,986,510
Florida	12,937,926
Pennsylvania	11,881,643

SOURCE: *United States Census Bureau*

1. Which state has the highest population? How many people live in that state? California; 29,760,021 people

2. Which two states are the closest in population? New York and Texas, with a difference of 1,003,945 people

3. How many more people live in California than live in Florida? 16,822,095

4. Are the combined populations of Texas and Florida greater than or less than the population of New York? greater than; 29,924,436 to 17,990,455

5. Which state do you think is likely to have the most professional sports teams? Why? California; because there are more people available to watch the games

NAME _____ DATE _____

B R I D G I N G   T H E   G A P

Solve a Word Puzzle

DIRECTIONS: Find the correct words to fill in the blanks in the following paragraph. Then write each word in the correct numbered space in the bridge puzzle below.

A **(8)** ROUTE _____ is a path from one place to another. A place where two routes cross is called a **(3)** CROSSROADS _____. A road built over a waterway is called a **(1)** BRIDGE _____. A **(9)** FERRY _____ is a boat that carries people and goods across a waterway. A **(10)** FORD _____ is a shallow place in a waterway that can be used as a crossing. London Bridge stretched across the **(2)** THAMES _____ River in **(6)** ENGLAND _____. Farmers would bring their goods from the countryside in **(7)** WAGONS _____ to **(11)** TRADE _____ for goods from ships. Today London Bridge has been moved to Lake **(4)** HAVASU _____ City, in **(5)** ARIZONA _____.

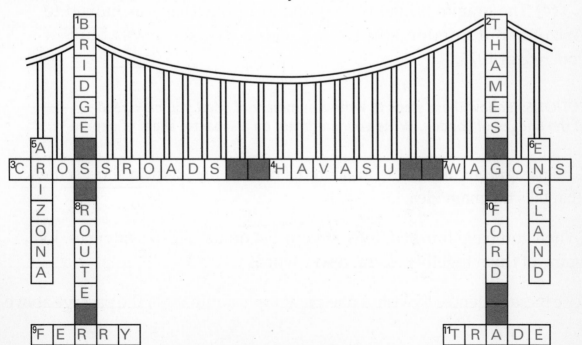

HOW TO WRITE A Summary

Apply Reading and Research Skills

DIRECTIONS: Read this passage about the bridges of London.

(1) The oldest London Bridge was probably built by Roman soldiers. It was made of boats tied together to stretch across the Thames River.

(2) In 1176 the people of London built a new London Bridge from stone. This London Bridge was famous. No one had ever built a bridge across such a big river in a city. Houses, shops, and even a church were built right on the bridge.

(3) As more buildings were added to the bridge, it began to crumble. Houses tilted. Bricks and roof tiles fell off and hit people in boats below. This was the bridge in the song, "London Bridge Is Falling Down." In 1831 it was replaced with a bridge made of granite, a very hard rock.

(4) The granite bridge is the London Bridge that was moved to Arizona. But London still has a London Bridge. It was built of concrete in 1973.

DIRECTIONS: Follow these steps to write a summary of what you have read about the bridges of London. Write your summary on a separate sheet of paper.

1. The paragraphs above are numbered. For each one, write a short sentence that tells the main idea.

2. When you have finished, look at your list of main idea sentences. Join some of them together, using fewer words.

3. Use these sentences to write a one-paragraph summary of the passage above.

Use after reading Unit 2, Skill Lesson, page 106.

❧ A Tale of Two Cities ❧

Organize Information

DIRECTIONS: *Some sentences in the list below apply to Cahokia. Other sentences apply to St. Louis. Some sentences apply to both cities. Write the number of each sentence in the correct part of the chart.*

Sentences

1. It was built where the Missouri River flows into the Mississippi River.

2. René Auguste Chouteau built a trading post here.

3. This city was built nearly 1,500 years ago.

4. It became an important trading center.

5. James Eads built a bridge here.

6. The Gateway Arch is a symbol of its past.

7. This city of 40,000 people vanished for an unknown reason.

8. It was named for a French king.

9. People here grew corn, beans, and squash on the riverbank.

10. Floods have caused problems.

CAHOKIA	BOTH	ST. LOUIS
3.	1.	2.
7.	4.	5.
9.	10.	6.
		8.

NAME _____ DATE _____

 Apply Map and Globe Skills

DIRECTIONS: Use this map to answer the questions below.

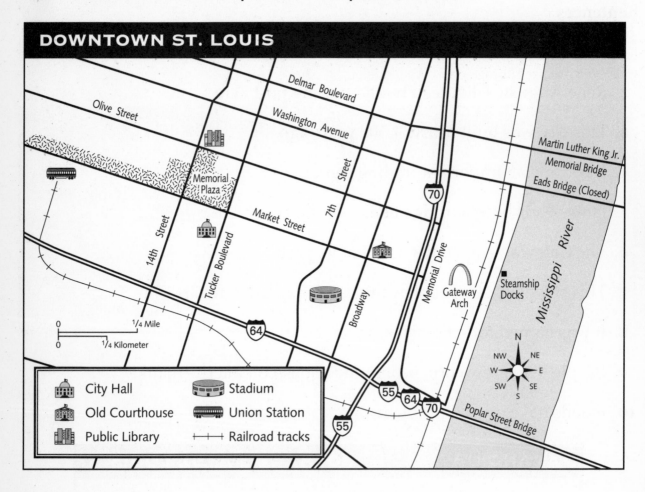

DOWNTOWN ST. LOUIS

In which direction would you travel to get from . . .

1. City Hall to Eads Bridge? ___northeast___

2. the Old Courthouse to the Stadium? ___southwest___

3. the Eads Bridge to Union Station? ___west___

4. the Gateway Arch to the Public Library? ___northwest___

a Resource

Use Creative Writing

DIRECTIONS: *Imagine that you are a natural resource. (If you need a suggestion, look in the Idea Box.) On the lines below, write about yourself. Be sure to tell what you are used for. Use as many interesting details as possible in your writing.*

IDEA BOX

Some natural resources

trees   water   soil

gold   silver   iron

oil   coal   animals

Look for factual accuracy and creative presentation in responses.

_____

_____

_____

_____

_____

_____

_____

_____

HOW TO USE A PRODUCT MAP

Apply Map and Globe Skills

DIRECTIONS: Study the map below. Then answer the questions below the map.

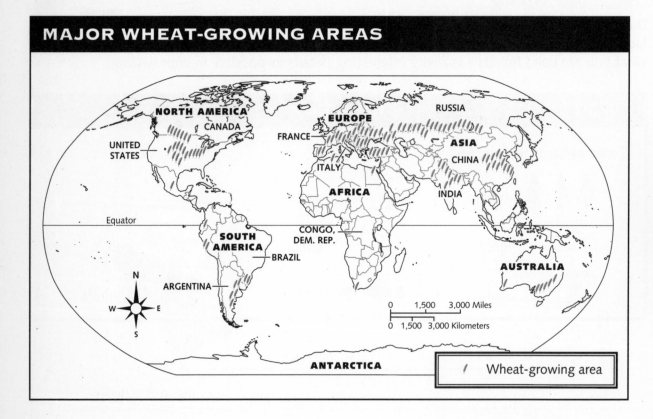

MAJOR WHEAT-GROWING AREAS

1. Not including Antarctica, which continent has the fewest wheat-producing areas? Africa

2. Does the United States or Australia have more wheat-producing areas?

the United States

3. Which country is more likely to have a wheat-milling industry, France or Brazil? Why? France; because it has a large area where wheat is grown

Capital Monuments

A monument is a statue or public building that honors a famous person or event. Here are some of the famous monuments you could see in Washington, D.C.

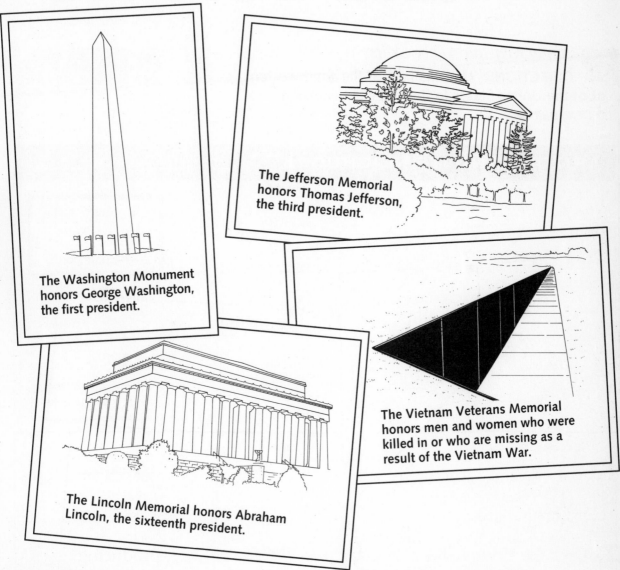

The Washington Monument honors George Washington, the first president.

The Jefferson Memorial honors Thomas Jefferson, the third president.

The Lincoln Memorial honors Abraham Lincoln, the sixteenth president.

The Vietnam Veterans Memorial honors men and women who were killed in or who are missing as a result of the Vietnam War.

Express Ideas in Art

DIRECTIONS: Think of a person or an idea that is important to your community. On a separate sheet of paper, design a monument to honor that person or idea.

HOW TO FIND
State Capitals and Borders

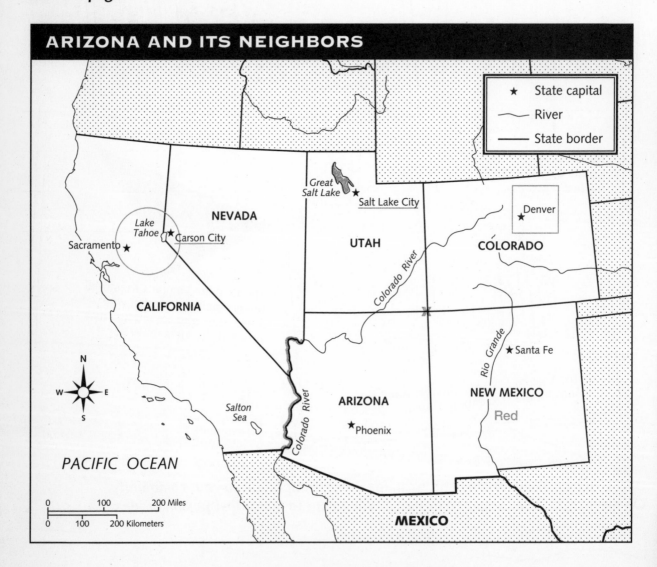

Apply Map and Globe Skills

DIRECTIONS: Use this map of the southwestern part of the United States to finish the activities on the next page.

ARIZONA AND ITS NEIGHBORS

Legend:
★ State capital
⌒ River
— State border

NEVADA
Great Salt Lake
★ Salt Lake City
Denver
Lake Tahoe
★ Carson City
Sacramento ★
UTAH
COLORADO
Colorado River
CALIFORNIA
X
Rio Grande
★ Santa Fe
N W E S
Salton Sea
Colorado River
ARIZONA
NEW MEXICO
Red
★ Phoenix
PACIFIC OCEAN

0   100   200 Miles
0   100   200 Kilometers

MEXICO

(Continued)

NAME _____ DATE _____

1. Underline all the state capitals that contain the word *City*.

2. Trace over the places where a river forms part of a state's border.

3. There is one place in the United States where you can stand in four states at once. Find this place on the map and mark it with an **X**.

4. Draw a circle around the two state capitals that are closest to each other.

5. Find a lake that has the same name as a state capital. Color the lake blue.

6. Santa Fe (FAY) is the oldest capital city in the United States. Find the state whose capital is Santa Fe. Color that state red.

7. Find the state that borders Utah to the east. Put a square around its capital.

8. What nation borders the United States to the south?

   Mexico
   _____

9. Name the five states the Colorado River touches. Colorado, Utah, Nevada, Arizona,

   California
   _____

10. Which state capital is closest to the Pacific Ocean? Sacramento
   _____

Building
BRASÍLIA

Recall and Reflect on the Lesson

DIRECTIONS: The sentences below contain some incorrect words. Read each sentence. Cross out the wrong word or words. Write the correct word or words above what you crossed out.

1. The city of Brasília sits high on a huge ~~hill~~ *plateau* in the middle of Brazil.

2. Brazil is the largest country in ~~Europe~~ *South America*.

3. Rio de Janeiro is known for its sandy ~~rivers~~ *beaches* and high ~~lakes~~ *mountains*.

4. Brazil is about as large as the ~~state of Rhode Island~~ *United States*.

5. A huge ~~ice~~ *rain* forest covers much of Brazil.

6. The ~~Nile~~ *Amazon* is Brazil's longest river. Only the ~~Mississippi~~ *Nile* River in Africa is longer.

7. All the materials to build Brasília had to be brought in by ~~tractors~~ *airplanes*.

DIRECTIONS: Read the paragraph about Brasília. Think carefully about the question that follows. Then write your answer on a separate sheet of paper. Give at least one reason for your answer.

The city of Brasília was built to get people to move to the center of the country. Brazil's coastal cities are crowded and polluted. But building cities in the rain forest can damage important natural resources. Trees in the rain forest help supply the oxygen we breathe. Rain forest plants provide many lifesaving medicines.

Do you think more cities like Brasília should be built in the rain forest?

Look for evidence of critical thinking on this issue.

NAME _____ DATE _____

WHERE PEOPLE START COMMUNITIES

Connect Main Ideas

DIRECTIONS: Use this organizer to show that you understand how the unit's main ideas are connected. Complete this graphic organizer by writing the main idea of each lesson.

Lesson 1
Communities are in different places.
People build communities in
places with many different
physical features.

Lesson 7
Communities move—Brasília, Brazil.
The capital was moved from Rio
to Brasília so it would be closer
to the center of the country.

Lesson 2
Communities are built near water.
Flowing water makes it easy
to ship goods and to receive
goods from far away.

Lesson 6
Communities are built for government.
Location is one thing leaders
think about when they decide
where to build a capital.

Where People Start Communities

Lesson 3
Communities are built where people meet.
Some cities and towns are
started at a crossroads, a
place where two routes meet

Lesson 5
Communities are built near resources.
People may settle in very hot
or cold climates in order to be
near the resources they need.

Lesson 4
Why did people build Cahokia and St. Louis?
People built Cahokia and
St. Louis along a riverbank,
where the soil was good and
where water could be used
for transportation.

Anchorage, Alaska

Use a Time Line to Show Change

DIRECTIONS: Use the time line below to answer the questions that follow it.

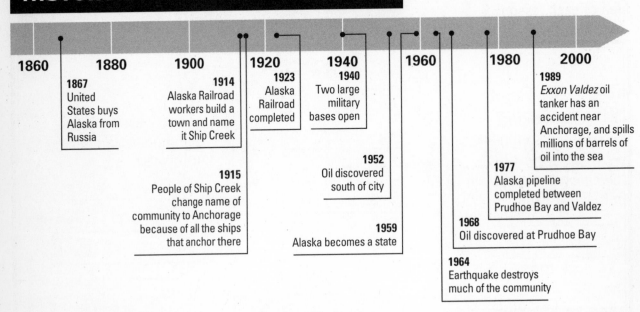

HISTORY OF ANCHORAGE, ALASKA

1860 · 1880 · 1900 · 1920 · 1940 · 1960 · 1980 · 2000

1867 United States buys Alaska from Russia

1914 Alaska Railroad workers build a town and name it Ship Creek

1915 People of Ship Creek change name of community to Anchorage because of all the ships that anchor there

1923 Alaska Railroad completed

1940 Two large military bases open

1952 Oil discovered south of city

1959 Alaska becomes a state

1964 Earthquake destroys much of the community

1968 Oil discovered at Prudhoe Bay

1977 Alaska pipeline completed between Prudhoe Bay and Valdez

1989 *Exxon Valdez* oil tanker has an accident near Anchorage, and spills millions of barrels of oil into the sea

1. When was the community given the name of Anchorage? 1915 _____

2. What happened to the city in 1964? An earthquake destroyed the community. _____

3. When was oil first discovered in the area? 1952 _____

4. When did Alaska become a state? 1959 _____

5. What might have led to a change in the population of the city in 1940?

the establishment of two military bases _____

6. What do you think might have been the effect of the discovery of oil in

the area? increase in jobs; growth of city in terms of population and businesses; impact on

environment _____

HOW TO COMPARE
Maps from Different Times

 *Apply Map and Globe Skills*

DIRECTIONS: Study the two maps of Boston on this page. Then answer the questions on the next page.

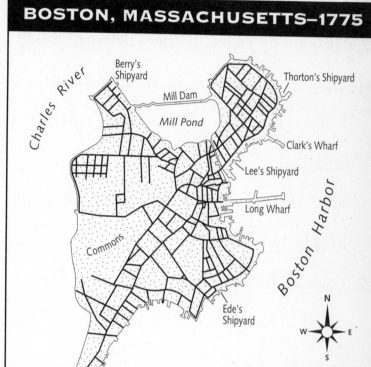

BOSTON, MASSACHUSETTS–1775

Charles River
Berry's Shipyard
Mill Dam
Mill Pond
Thorton's Shipyard
Clark's Wharf
Lee's Shipyard
Long Wharf
Boston Harbor
Commons
Ede's Shipyard

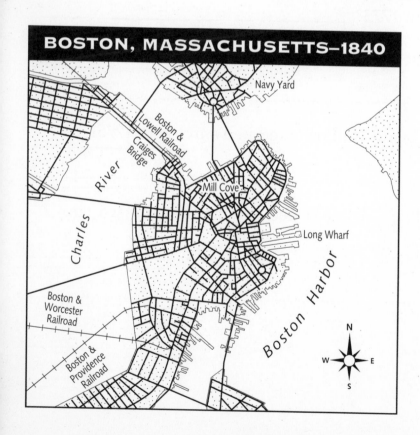

BOSTON, MASSACHUSETTS–1840

Navy Yard
Boston & Lowell Railroad
Craiges Bridge
River
Mill Cove
Charles
Long Wharf
Boston Harbor
Boston & Worcester Railroad
Boston & Providence Railroad

(Continued)

NAME _____ DATE _____

1. What is the date of the first map? 1775 _____

2. What is the date of the second map? 1840 _____

3. How many years are there between the time periods of the two maps?

   65 years _____

4. What is the name of the longest wharf on both maps?

   Long Wharf _____

5. Find Mill Dam on the older map. What physical feature is south of

   Mill Dam? Mill Pond _____

6. Look at the more recent map and tell what happened to this

   physical feature. It was filled in and became living space called Mill Cove. _____

   _____

7. Were there any railroads in 1775? no _____

8. In 1840, over which bridge did the Boston & Lowell Railroad pass?

   Craiges Bridge _____

9. How do you think many people in Boston earned a living in 1775?

   working in the shipyards _____

10. Do you think some people in Boston earned a living the same way in

    1840? Explain your answer. Yes; the map shows a Navy Yard. _____

    _____

Use after reading Unit 3, Skill Lesson, pages 162–163.

The Hoopas and the Cheyennes

Solve a Word Puzzle

DIRECTIONS: Use the clues below to solve the puzzle on the next page.

CLUES

Down

1. Indian group that lived in northeastern California

2. animal that changed the Cheyennes' way of life

3. Hoopas, Karoks, and Yuroks did this with one another to get the things they needed or wanted

4. Hoopas made these into hats and cradles

5. food for Hoopas that came from the water

Across

2. the Cheyennes began to _____ instead of farm

4. animal used by the Cheyennes for food, clothing, and homes

6. Cheyenne home

7. Indian group that lived in the Great Plains

8. Hoopa homes

(Continued)

Use after reading Unit 3, Lesson 2, pages 164-170.

The Aztecs

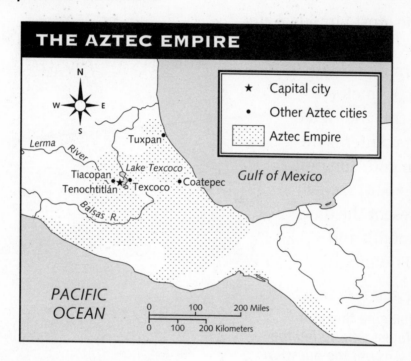

🌐 *Learn from a Map*

DIRECTIONS: Study the map of the Aztec Empire below. Then answer the questions that follow.

THE AZTEC EMPIRE

★ Capital city
• Other Aztec cities
⋮ Aztec Empire

N · W · E · S

Lerma River
Tuxpan
Tiacopan
Lake Texcoco
Tenochtitlán · Texcoco · Coatepec
Balsas R.
Gulf of Mexico

PACIFIC OCEAN

0   100   200 Miles
0 100 200 Kilometers

1. Near what physical feature were most Aztec cities built?

Lake Texcoco

2. What was the capital city of the Aztecs? Tenochtitlán

3. Between what two bodies of water was the Aztec Empire located?

the Gulf of Mexico and the Pacific Ocean

4. What was the northernmost Aztec city? Tuxpan

5. What was the westernmost Aztec city? Tiacopan

6. What two rivers flowed through part of the Aztec Empire?

Lerma and Balsas rivers

HOW TO LEARN from Artifacts

One of the most famous Aztec artifacts is the Calendar Stone. This stone, which measures about 12 feet (about 3.7 meters) across, represents the Aztec universe. In its center is the face of the sun god, Tonatiuh (toh•nah•TEE•ooh). Other carvings represent the days of the Aztec month and show religious symbols.

Apply Reading and Research Skills

DIRECTIONS: Imagine that you are the archaeologist who found the Calendar Stone. Answer the questions below by studying the artifact and using the information about the Aztecs in your textbook.

1. Where do you think this artifact was found? Mexico _____

2. Why do you think it was made from stone? Stone was at hand and is long-lasting. _____

_____

3. How do you think people used this artifact? The calendar was used to keep track

of the seasons and the days. _____

4. What else can you learn about Aztec culture from the Calendar Stone?

Answers will vary but should indicate that the Aztecs were artistic, had the tools that allowed them

to shape and carve stones, practiced religious ceremonies, etc.

Use after reading Unit 3, Skill Lesson, page 175.

Mexico City: Cleaning the Air

Summarize Information

DIRECTIONS: Use the information in Lesson 4 of your textbook to complete the graphic organizer below. In each of the four lower clouds, write one way that the people of Mexico City are trying to solve their air-pollution problem.

Solving Mexico City's Air-Pollution Problem

Closing of some factories

"No driving today" laws

Vehicles that use special fuels and engines

Use of public transportation

HOW TO SOLVE A PROBLEM

Apply Participation Skills

DIRECTIONS: Read the story below. Then answer the questions that follow.

The first day of fishing season is always an exciting time. Everyone goes to his or her favorite fishing place to see how many fish he or she can catch. Last year Will caught six fish! That was more than anyone else caught. This year we all wanted to beat Will's record. George, Jamal, Emily, and I went to a small pond in Jones Park. What we saw there shocked us all. There was garbage all along the edge of the pond. Garbage cans had been overturned, and aluminum cans were all over the place. Plastic garbage bags and plastic containers were floating on top of the pond. Emily even found a few dead fish that had washed up onto land. Fishing quickly became the furthest thing from our minds. We had to come up with a way to save this pond!

1. What problem have these children identified? People are littering and fish
are dying.

2. What are some possible solutions to the problem? Responses might include
cleaning the park or having the police patrol the park.

3. What are the good and the bad points of your possible solutions?
Good: the park will look better; police patrols will reduce problems. Bad: the cleanup might only be
temporary; police could be more effectively used doing other things.

4. How would you carry out your solutions? ask friends for help; talk to town officials;
call the police

5. What would you do to see if your solutions were working?
visit the park regularly to see if solutions are working

Use after reading Unit 3, Skill Lesson, pages 180–181.

Our Country's Early History

Apply Information

DIRECTIONS: Read the statements below. If the statement is true, write a T on the line. If it is false, write an F on the line. Cross out the part that is false, and make the statement true.

George Washington

Abraham Lincoln

T **1.** South Carolina left the Union.

F **2.** ~~French~~ English settlers founded Jamestown.

T **3.** John Adams, Benjamin Franklin, and Thomas Jefferson wrote the Declaration of Independence.

F **4.** Colonists threw ~~coffee~~ tea into Boston Harbor.

F **5.** The Civil War took place between the ~~East~~ North and the ~~West~~ South.

F **6.** The first people brought to the colonies as slaves came from ~~China~~ Africa.

T **7.** George Washington became the first President.

T **8.** Abraham Lincoln helped pass the Thirteenth Amendment.

F **9.** The colonies fought against ~~Spain~~ England for freedom.

F **10.** The Constitution was written by people in ~~England~~ the thirteen colonies.

Changing Inventions

New inventions often cause changes in the way people in communities live and work. Sometimes the inventions themselves change over the years.

Place Items in Order

DIRECTIONS: Shown below are nine drawings. Under each drawing, place a T for Telephone, an A for Automobile, or a W for Writing Tool. Then go back and place a 1, 2, or 3 in each category to show the order in which you think the objects were invented.

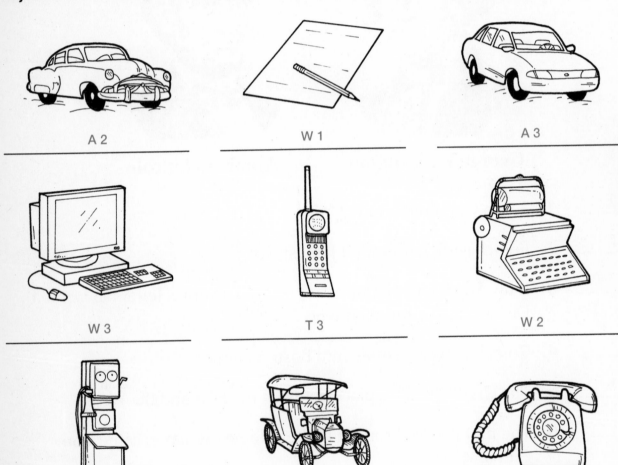

A 2   W 1   A 3

W 3   T 3   W 2

T 1   A 1   T 2

Critical Thinking

DIRECTIONS: On a separate sheet of paper, describe a new invention that you think will cause a change in your community.

A Time Line of Houston, Texas

Houston has more people than any other city in Texas. Only three cities in the United States have more people.

Determine Order

DIRECTIONS: Below is a list of events in the history of Houston, Texas. Write these events in their proper order on the time line.

1836: Houston founded
1914: Ship channel to the Gulf of Mexico completed
1876: First free public schools started
1859: Fire destroys city's business district
1901: Oil discovered
1853: Area's first railroad started
1891: Streetcars first used

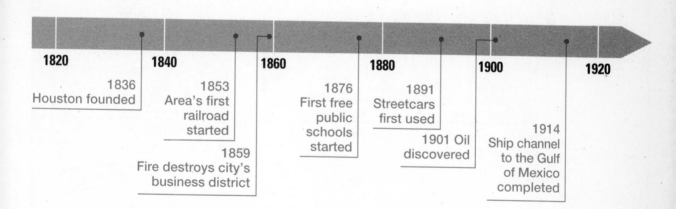

1820

1840

1860

1880

1900

1920

1836
Houston founded

1853
Area's first
railroad
started

1876
First free
public
schools
started

1891
Streetcars
first used

1901 Oil
discovered

1914
Ship channel
to the Gulf
of Mexico
completed

1859
Fire destroys city's
business district

COMMUNITIES *Grow and Change*

Connect Main Ideas

DIRECTIONS: Use this organizer to show that you understand how the unit's main ideas are connected. Complete this graphic organizer by writing the main idea for each lesson.

Communities Grow and Change

Lesson 1
Communities change yet stay the same.
An old building is torn down. A new building takes its place.

Lesson 2
Some Native American communities changed while others did not.
The geographic location of the Hoopas helped their way of life stay much the same. When the Cheyennes began using horses, their way of life changed.

Lesson 3
Aztec communities grew and changed long ago.
Tenochtitlán changed from the capital of the Aztec Empire to present-day Mexico City.

Lesson 5
People moved from England and settled in what is now the United States.
The colonists' fought for freedom from British rule. Throughout our country's history, the idea of freedom has always been important.

Lesson 4
Change in a community can create problems.
Large cities often may have pollution problems.

Lesson 6
Inventions change communication and transportation.
Inventions such as the telegraph, telephone, computer, automobile, airplane, rocket, and space shuttle changed the way people communicated and traveled.

Lesson 7
Every community has a history.
Family members and workers in your community can tell you how to find information about your community.

Use after reading Unit 3, pages 140–207.

Lancaster, Pennsylvania

Locate Places on a Map

DIRECTIONS: Many Amish communities in the United States are located in Lancaster County, Pennsylvania. Study the map below of the downtown area of the city of Lancaster. Then complete the activities that follow.

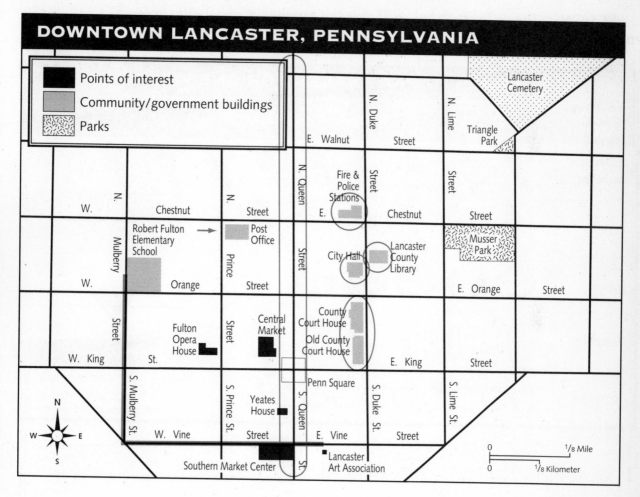

DOWNTOWN LANCASTER, PENNSYLVANIA

Points of interest
Community/government buildings
Parks

1. From Penn Square, travel one block west, and then two blocks north. Draw an arrow pointing to the building on your right.

2. Trace the route you would take from the Lancaster Art Association to Robert Fulton Elementary School.

3. Circle all the community government buildings on Duke Street.

4. Circle the length of the street that divides Lancaster into east and west streets.

HOW TO READ GRAPHS

Apply Chart and Graph Skills

DIRECTIONS: The pictograph below shows the number of vegetables sold at Josh's Market. Use the graph to answer the questions that follow.

JOSH'S MARKET SALES FOR ONE WEEK	
TYPE OF VEGETABLE	**NUMBER OF VEGETABLES SOLD**
Asparagus (bunches)	🌿🌿🌿🌿🌿🌿🌿🌿🌿
Corn	🌽🌽🌽🌽🌽🌽
Lettuce	🥬🥬🥬🥬🥬
Pumpkins	🎃🎃🎃🎃🎃🎃
Tomatoes	🍅🍅🍅🍅🍅🍅🍅🍅🍅🍅

KEY
Each symbol equals 5 vegetables sold

1. How many heads of lettuce were sold? _25 heads of lettuce_

2. Which vegetable did Josh sell the most of? How many did he sell?

tomatoes; 50 tomatoes

3. Which two vegetables sold in equal amounts? How many of each were sold?

corn and pumpkins; 30 of each

4. If Josh wanted to show on this graph that he sold 20 bunches of asparagus, how many asparagus symbols would he show? _4 symbols_

Use after reading Unit 4, Skill Lesson, page 226.

Developing a Product

The development of a product requires bringing together technology, human resources, raw materials, and a means of transportation.

Classify Information

DIRECTIONS: The center circle in the diagram below provides a list of words. Group, or classify, these words into one of the four categories shown in the smaller circles.

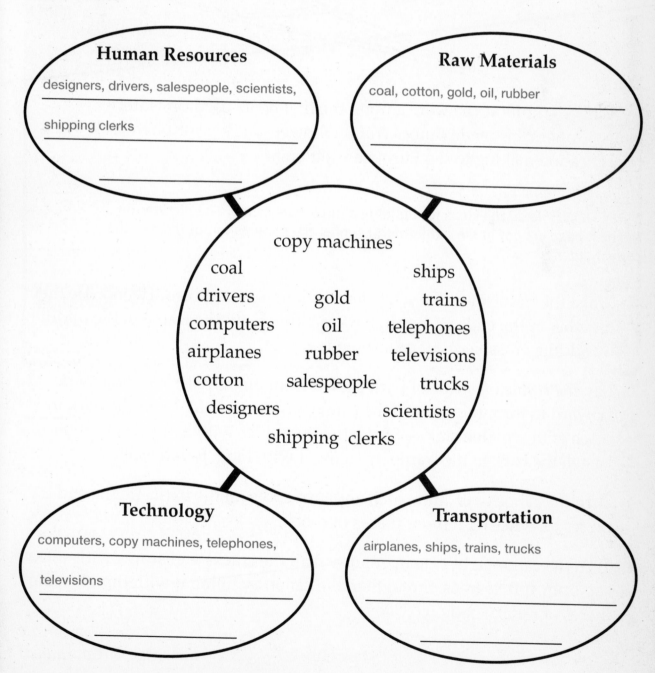

Human Resources

designers, drivers, salespeople, scientists, _____

shipping clerks _____

_____

Raw Materials

coal, cotton, gold, oil, rubber _____

_____

_____

copy machines

coal · ships

drivers · gold · trains

computers · oil · telephones

airplanes · rubber · televisions

cotton · salespeople · trucks

designers · scientists

shipping clerks

Technology

computers, copy machines, telephones, _____

televisions _____

_____

Transportation

airplanes, ships, trains, trucks _____

_____

_____

HOW TO USE A FLOW CHART

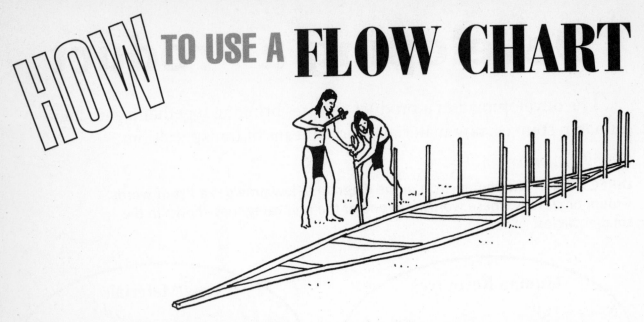

Canoes (kuh•NOOZ) were among the first boats used on waterways. Native Americans made canoes from hollowed-out logs or birch bark. They taught canoe-making to the European settlers.

Apply Chart and Graph Skills

DIRECTIONS: Read the steps for building a birch-bark canoe. The pictures on the next page are not in the right order. Number the pictures to put them in the correct order.

1. Make the frame of the canoe from two long pieces of cedarwood. Tie them together at the ends with tough roots. Stretch out the frame in the middle by adding crosspieces of cedarwood.

2. Lay the frame on strips of bark peeled from birch trees. Wrap the bark upward to form the sides of the canoe, inside and out. Hold the bark in place with wooden stakes. Strengthen the sides with extra sheets of bark. Fasten the bark to the frame by lacing it with long, tough roots.

3. Turn the canoe over, and patch any torn spots on the bark. Tie the end pieces together with more pieces of roots.

4. Turn the canoe right side up, and seal all the cracks and seams with sticky sap from spruce trees. Strengthen the canoe by lining it with thin, flexible pieces of cedarwood.

(Continued)

  Use after reading Unit 4, Skill Lesson, pages 232–233.

a. __3__

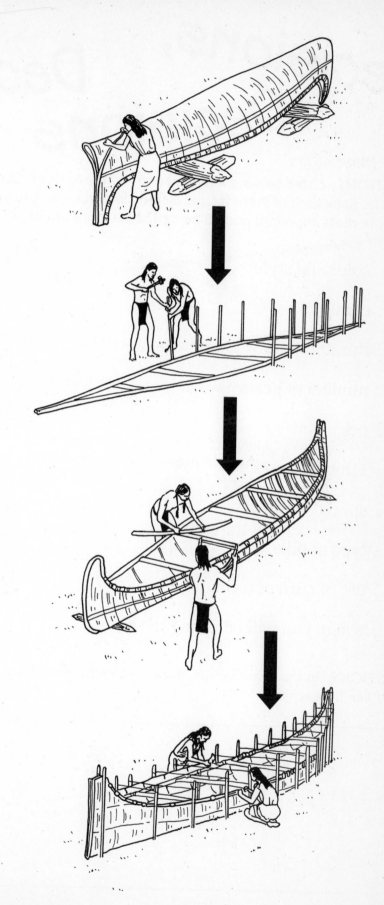

b. __1__

c. __4__

d. __2__

Decisions, Decisions, Decisions

Apply Information

DIRECTIONS: Listed below are a number of things to think about when buying a bicycle. Rank each of these factors by how important it is to you, with 1 being the most important and 10 being the least important.

_____ color and style

_____ comfort

_____ durability (how long the bike will last)

_____ number of gears

_____ price

_____ safety features

_____ special features

_____ type of bike

_____ use of current technology

_____ where you will be riding the bike

DIRECTIONS: In the space below, draw an advertisement for a bicycle that you would like to purchase.

HOW TO MAKE AN Economic Choice

Apply Critical Thinking Skills

DIRECTIONS: Kate decided she wanted to have new ice skates before winter. Her parents told her she must pay half the cost of the skates. Listed below are several choices she made. If the choice helped her reach her goal of buying the skates, put a + sign in the blank. If the choice did not help her reach her goal, put a - sign in the blank.

__+__ **1.** Kate takes care of a neighbor's dog while the woman is on a business trip. Kate earns $5.00 and puts it in her bank.

__-__ **2.** Kate and her cousins go to the beach with her aunt. Even though her aunt brought lemonade, Kate buys a soft drink from the soda machine.

__-__ **3.** Her best friend is having a slumber party. Kate buys a new sleep shirt just for the party.

__+__ **4.** Kate puts her allowance in her bank every week.

__+__ **5.** Grandmother sends her $10.00 for her birthday. Kate puts it in her bank.

__-__ **6.** Kate forgets her lunch one day and buys a sandwich at school.

__+__ **7.** Kate's older brother helps her collect aluminum cans. They split the money they get at the recycling station. Kate puts her money in her bank.

Let's Make a DEAL!

Understand What You Read

DIRECTIONS: In the literature selection Saturday Sancocho you learned how Maria Lili and her grandmother bartered to get the things they needed for a special stew. Read the story below about one of America's most famous barter deals. Then answer the questions that follow.

In 1624 a number of families from the Netherlands, a country in northwestern Europe, came to North America. They settled along the Hudson River. The leader of the group was Peter Minuit (MIN•yuh•wut). The land Minuit and his followers settled on, however, was already occupied by Native Americans. Peter Minuit offered to trade about $24 worth of trinkets, beads, and knives for the entire island of Manhattan. The Native Americans accepted Minuit's trade, not fully understanding that they had sold the land. As a result of this deal, the people from the Netherlands ended up owning a large part of what we know today as New York City for a cost of only about $24.

1. What did Peter Minuit offer the Native Americans for the island

of Manhattan? about $24 worth of trinkets, beads, and knives

2. Do you think this was a fair offer? Why? Answers will vary, but some may note that

it was not a fair offer because the Indians did not fully understand that they had sold the land.

3. If a group of explorers discovered some undeveloped land today, what might they offer the people for that land?

Answers might include medical supplies, portable electronic gadgets, money, and so on.

Use after reading Unit 4, Lesson 4, pages 242–249.

HOW TO USE A Map Grid

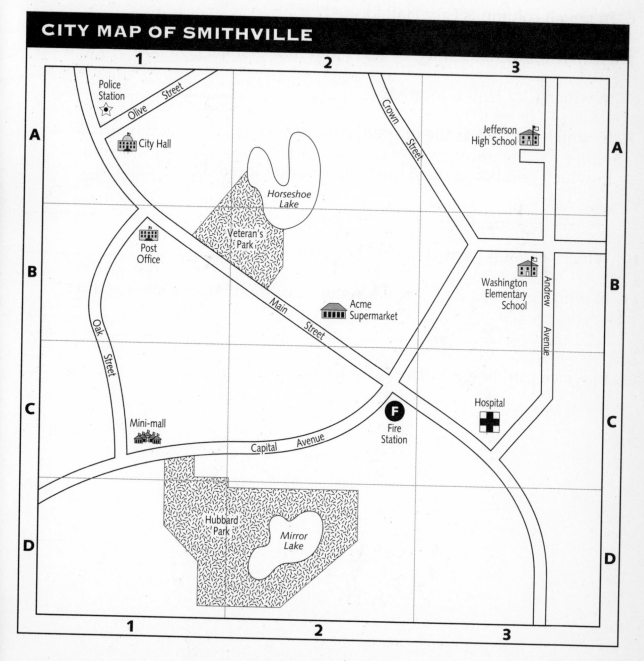

Apply Map and Globe Skills

DIRECTIONS: Use the map and grid shown below to answer the questions on the next page.

CITY MAP OF SMITHVILLE

(Continued)

1. How many rows are shown on this map? *4 rows* _____

2. How are the rows labeled? *by the letters A, B, C, and D* _____

3. How many columns are shown on this map? *3 columns* _____

4. How are the columns labeled? *by the numbers 1, 2, and 3* _____

5. In which row is City Hall located? *row A* _____

6. In which column is City Hall located? *column 1* _____

7. How would you identify, by letter and number, the grid box

   in which City Hall is located? *A-1* _____

8. In which grid box is the hospital located? *C-3* _____

9. In which grid box is the Acme Supermarket located?

   B-2 _____

10. Which school is located in grid box A-3? *Jefferson High School* _____

11. In which grid box do Capital Avenue and Main Street come together?

    C-2 _____

12. In which grid box is Mirror Lake located? *D-2* _____

Use after reading Unit 4, Skill Lesson, pages 250–251.

Major Ports

Interpret Information from a Graph

DIRECTIONS: Examine the bar graph below. Then answer the questions that follow.

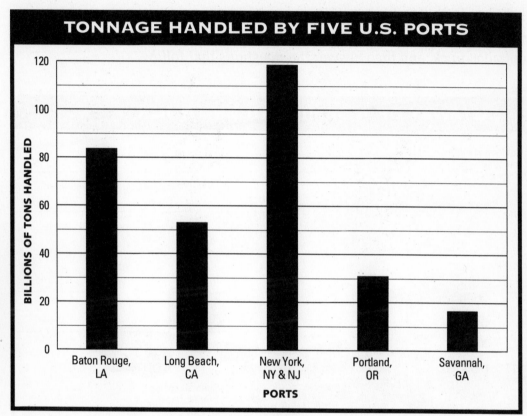

TONNAGE HANDLED BY FIVE U.S. PORTS

BILLIONS OF TONS HANDLED

Baton Rouge, LA — Long Beach, CA — New York, NY & NJ — Portland, OR — Savannah, GA

PORTS

SOURCE: *Statistical Abstract of the United States*

1. Which port handles the greatest amount of tonnage?

New York, NY & NJ

2. What is the amount of tonnage handled by Portland?

about 31 billion tons

3. Does Long Beach or Baton Rouge handle more tons of products?

Baton Rouge, LA

4. In tons, how much more does Portland handle than Savannah?

about 14 billion tons more

HOW TO READ
a Cutaway Diagram

Apply Chart and Graph Skills

DIRECTIONS: A cutaway diagram can help you see an object's parts. Study the cutaway diagram of a semitrailer-truck, and then answer the questions that follow.

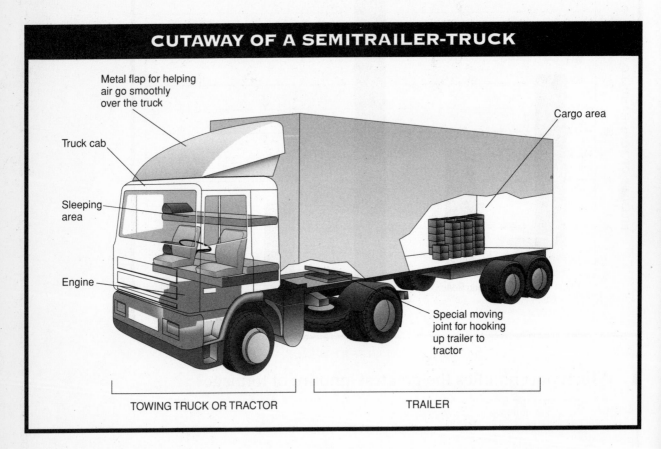

CUTAWAY OF A SEMITRAILER-TRUCK

Metal flap for helping air go smoothly over the truck

Truck cab

Sleeping area

Engine

Cargo area

Special moving joint for hooking up trailer to tractor

TOWING TRUCK OR TRACTOR

TRAILER

1. Where is the sleeping area located? in the truck cab, above and behind the seats

2. What is the special moving joint used for? to attach the trailer to the tractor

3. In what part of the truck are products hauled? in the cargo area of the trailer

4. Where is the engine located? in the tractor under the seats

5. What does the metal flap above the truck cab do? helps air go smoothly over

the truck

Use after reading Unit 4, Skill Lesson, pages 258–259.

People Working Together

Connect Main Ideas

DIRECTIONS: Use this organizer to show that you understand how the unit's main ideas are connected. Complete this graphic organizer by writing details for the main idea of each lesson.

Lesson 1
People in a community work together.
1. People in the Amish community work together to meet their needs.
2. People in all communities need to buy products they cannot make and services they cannot provide.

Lesson 5
Products and services get to marketplaces in different ways.
1. People can carry items _____ to marketplaces.
2. People can ship items _____ by train, truck, or boat

People Working Together

Lesson 2
People work together to make products and provide services.
1. People work together in factories to make bicycle helmets.
2. In a factory, work is done in steps to make a product.

Lesson 4
People trade, or barter, with each other.
1. People sometimes barter one thing for another.
2. In bartering, the traded items should be worth about the same amount.

Lesson 3
People choose the products and services they will buy.
1. People may read advertisements before they buy a product.
2. Consumers must decide if they want or need a product and how much money they can spend.

Questions About City Government

Summarize Information

DIRECTIONS: Use Lesson 1 of your textbook to answer each of the questions below about city government.

1. What can citizens do to request that an action be taken by their local government?

attend meetings of their town council

organize the preparation of a written petition

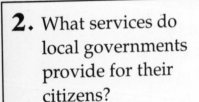

2. What services do local governments provide for their citizens?

fire and police protection

libraries

street and traffic signs

sewers, water

3. How do local governments get the money they need to provide services to the community?

through the collection

of taxes

HOW TO RESOLVE CONFLICTS

Apply Participation Skills

DIRECTIONS: Read the two situations below. On the lines provided, explain how you could deal with the conflict described. Use one or more of the steps outlined in the Resolve Conflicts skill in your textbook.

You just got a new bicycle for your birthday. It is a bright, sunny day, and you decide to take your bicycle out for a ride. On your way to show your bicycle to Tasha, you are stopped by Jimmy. He starts to make fun of you and your new bicycle. Jimmy tells you that as soon as he gets the chance he is going to wreck your new bicycle.

Answers will vary, but may include either or both of the following steps: walk (ride) away; ask

someone to help you.

_____

_____

You told Justin and Maurice you would meet them by the swings at the park. When you get there, your two friends are already playing on the swings. There is one swing not in use, so you head toward it. Just as you start to sit down, you are pushed away by a girl whom you have never seen before. She grabs the swing and begins to swing on it.

Answers will vary, but may include any or all of the following steps: walk away, compromise, or smile

about it.

_____

_____

The Bill of Rights

The Bill of Rights is the first ten additions made to the United States Constitution. These ten additions, or amendments, protect the rights and freedoms of all Americans.

Match Words and Pictures

DIRECTIONS: Below is a list of five of the freedoms or rights protected by the Bill of Rights. Draw a line between each of these freedoms and a drawing on the right that illustrates that freedom.

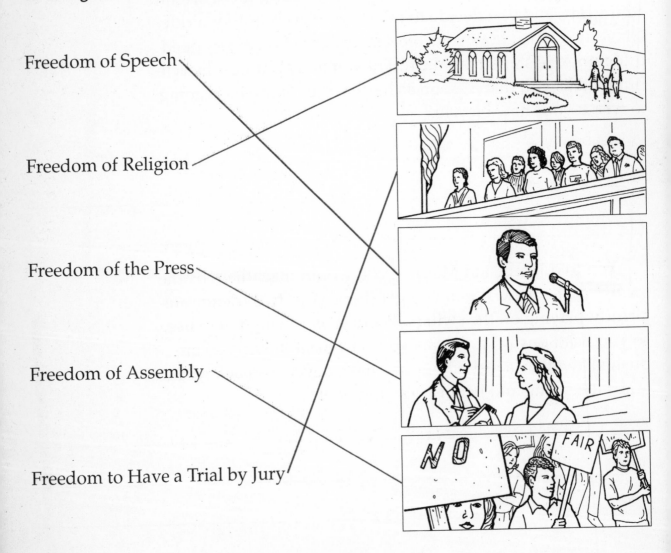

Freedom of Speech

Freedom of Religion

Freedom of the Press

Freedom of Assembly

Freedom to Have a Trial by Jury

Use after reading Unit 5, Lesson 2, pages 290–294.

HOW TO MAKE A CHOICE BY VOTING

Apply Participation Skills

DIRECTIONS: Review the Think and Apply section on page 297 of your textbook. Then fill in the fact sheet below to organize information about each candidate running in the school election. Use this information to help you decide whom to vote for.

Candidate's Name: _____

Ideas I agree with: Students' responses will vary. _____

_____

Ideas I disagree with: _____

_____

Why I would or would not vote for this candidate:_____

_____

Candidate's Name: _____

Ideas I agree with: Students' responses will vary. _____

_____

Ideas I disagree with: _____

_____

Why I would or would not vote for this candidate:_____

_____

Finding Your Way *THROUGH*
State Government

Identify State Services

DIRECTIONS: Make your way through the maze below by finding all the jobs done by state governments. Don't let your route pass through any services that are not provided by the state.

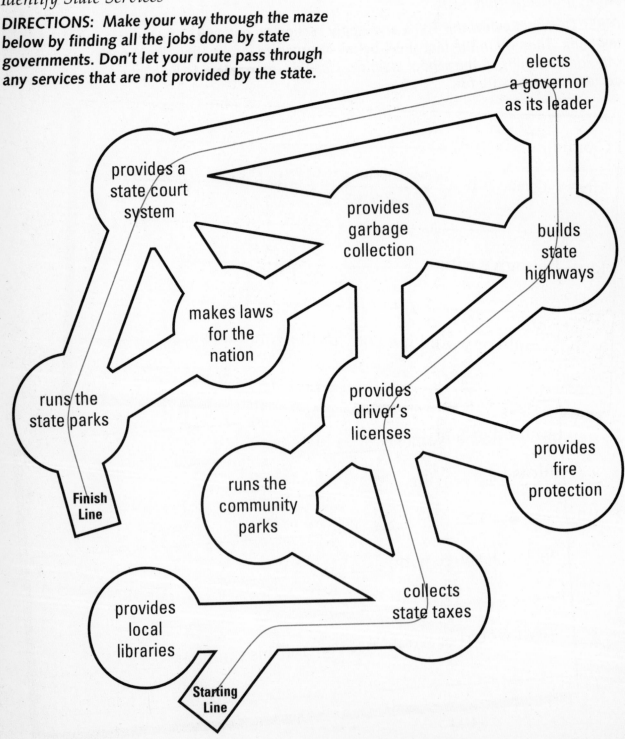

elects a governor as its leader

provides a state court system

provides garbage collection

builds state highways

makes laws for the nation

runs the state parks

provides driver's licenses

provides fire protection

Finish Line

runs the community parks

provides local libraries

collects state taxes

Starting Line

Use after reading Unit 5, Lesson 3, pages 298–301.

NAME _____   DATE _____

HOW TO MEASURE Distance on a Map

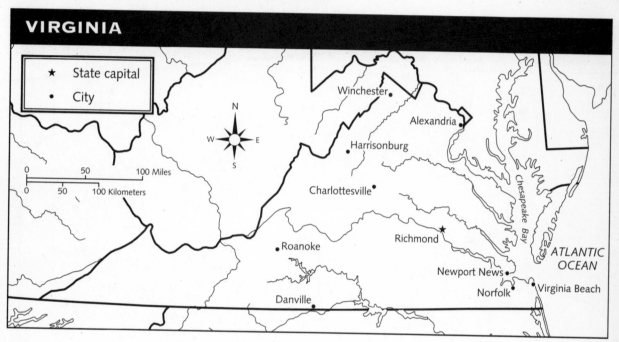

Apply Map and Globe Skills

DIRECTIONS: Use the distance scale on the map below to answer the questions that follow.

1. In miles, about how far is it from Richmond to Winchester?

about 120 miles

2. What is the distance in kilometers between Richmond and Winchester?

about 200 kilometers

3. How many miles long is the southern boundary of Virginia?

about 430 miles

4. What is the distance in kilometers between Winchester and Danville?

about 300 kilometers

Use after reading Unit 5, Skill Lesson, page 302.

ACTIVITY BOOK   59

THE House of Representatives

Map Skill

Analyze Information

DIRECTIONS: The map below shows the number of representatives that each state has in the House of Representatives. Examine the map. Then answer the questions that follow.

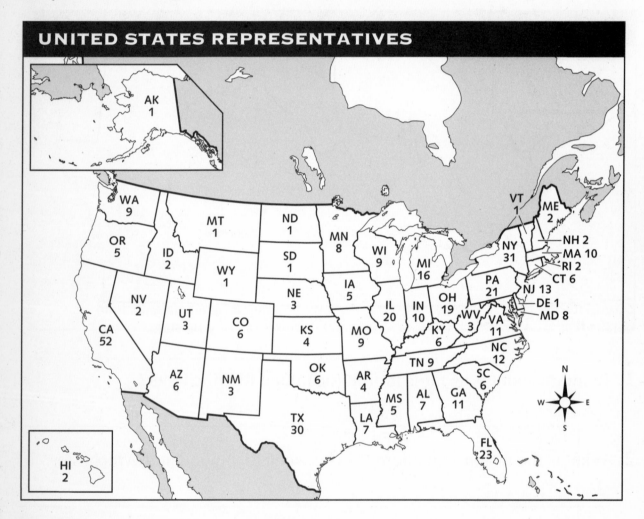

UNITED STATES REPRESENTATIVES

1. What state has the most people in the House of Representatives?

California

2. How many representatives does your state have? Answers will vary by state.

3. How many representatives does Texas have? 30 representatives

Design a **State Flag**

Create a Flag

DIRECTIONS: Each of the 50 states in the United States has its own flag. Below is Tennessee's state flag. Color it as indicated. Then answer the question.

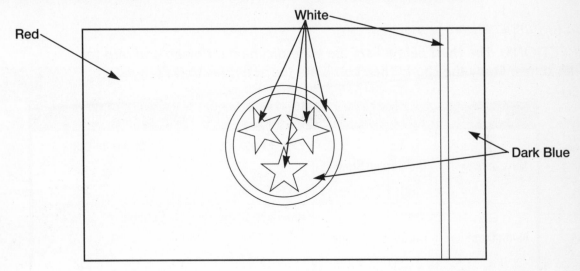

Why do you think this flag has three stars? Answer on a separate sheet of paper.
Accept reasonable responses: The three stars represent the three parts of Tennessee: Middle, Eastern, and Western.

DIRECTIONS: In the space below, design a new state flag for your state. Include details that tell something about the geography and history of your state.

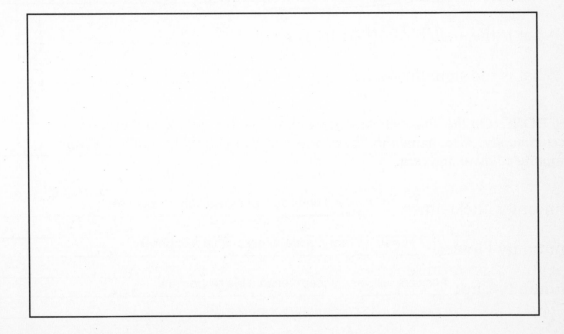

HOW TO COMPARE Patriotic Symbols

Apply Participation Skills

DIRECTIONS: The chart below lists the state nickname, flower, and bird for three states. Study the chart. Then complete the activities that follow.

STATE	NICKNAME	FLOWER	BIRD
New Jersey	The Garden State	Purple Violet	Eastern Goldfinch
North Carolina	The Tar Heel State	American Dogwood	Cardinal
California	The Golden State	Golden Poppy	California Valley Quail

1. Which state is known as the Golden State? _California_____

2. What is the state bird of North Carolina? _Cardinal_____

3. What is the state flower of New Jersey? _Purple Violet_____

DIRECTIONS: On the lines below, write a nickname that you would pick for your community. Also, name the flower and bird that you think should be your community's flower and bird.

Community Nickname: _Answers will vary; accept reasonable responses._____

Community Flower: _Answers will vary; accept reasonable responses._____

Community Bird: _Answers will vary; accept reasonable responses._____

Use after reading Unit 5, Skill Lesson, pages 316–319.

South Africa and the United States

Compare Information

DIRECTIONS: The table below compares South Africa and the United States. Study the table. Then answer the questions that follow.

	SOUTH AFRICA	UNITED STATES
Land Area	471,445 square miles (1,221,043 sq km)	3,536,341 square miles (9,159,123 sq km)
Population	42,327,458	267,636,061
Monetary Unit	Rand	Dollar
Largest City	Johannesburg	New York City
Political Divisions	9 provinces	50 states
Form of Government	Republic	Federal Republic

SOURCE: *The World Factbook; Webster's Geographical Dictionary*

1. Which country has a greater land area? What is the difference in the land area in square miles of the two countries? the United States; 3,064,896 square miles

_____

2. About how many times more people live in the United States than live in South Africa? About six times more people live in the United States.

_____

3. Now write a paragraph comparing South Africa and the United States. You may also include information from your textbook.

Paragraphs will vary, but should accurately use the information from the table and the textbook to

compare the two countries.

_____

_____

Living Together in a Community, State, and Nation

Connect Main Ideas

DIRECTIONS: Use this organizer to show that you understand how the unit's main ideas are connected. Complete the organizer by writing details for the main idea of each lesson.

Lesson 6
Solving problems in other countries
1. The leaders in South Africa wanted fair treatment for people of all races.
2. The leaders in South Africa wrote a new Constitution.

Lesson 1
Solving community problems
1. Citizens can ask community members to sign a petition.
2. Citizens can work with their local government to solve problems.

Lesson 5
Patriotic symbols
1. The national flag is a patriotic symbol.
2. The bald eagle is a national symbol used on the Great Seal of the United States.

Living Together in a Community, State, and Nation

Lesson 2
Rules and laws
1. Dekanawida made up a set of laws to help bring peace to the five Iroquois tribes.
2. The Pilgrims wrote a set of laws called the Mayflower Compact

Lesson 4
Branches of national government
1. The President leads the government and helps keep the country safe.
2. The President, Congress, and Supreme Court work together to do important jobs for the national government.

Lesson 3
State governments
1. Each state government has a governor to lead it.
2. The National Guard can help citizens in an emergency.

Use after reading Unit 5, pages 268–335.

THE STATUE OF LIBERTY

In 1883 Emma Lazarus wrote a poem called "The New Colossus." Some of the words from this poem were carved into the base of the Statue of Liberty in 1903.

Apply Writing Skills

DIRECTIONS: Read the words below that appear on the base of the Statue of Liberty. Then write your own poem of welcome for new immigrants to the United States.

> Give me your tired, your poor,
> Your huddled masses yearning to breathe free,
> The wretched refuse of your teeming shore.
> Send these, the homeless, tempest-tost to me,
> I lift my lamp beside the golden door!

Explain difficult words in the poem to students. After a

discussion about the poem, ask students to write their own

poems as directed. Students' poems will vary. Accept

rhyming or nonrhyming poems. As you evaluate the

poems, look for an understanding of the concepts

presented in Lesson 1.

_____

_____

_____

_____

_____

_____

DUKE ELLINGTON

Interpret Information

DIRECTIONS: Read the paragraph below about one of the world's greatest jazz musicians, Duke Ellington. Then answer the questions that follow.

Duke Ellington was born in 1899 in Washington, D.C. Duke Ellington wrote music, led bands, and played the piano. In the 1920s he moved from Washington, D.C., to live in Harlem, New York. His band played in concert halls, nightclubs, and theaters all over the world. Duke Ellington also wrote music for Broadway plays, motion pictures, and television shows. He wrote more than 1,500 songs. Much of Duke Ellington's music is now part of the Duke Ellington Collection at the Smithsonian Institution in Washington, D.C.

1. Why do you think Duke Ellington moved to Harlem, New York, in the 1920s? Answers should note that Ellington probably moved to Harlem to be part of the large and growing African American community of artists and musicians living there.

2. If you could ask Duke Ellington only one question, what would that question be? Explain why you would ask this question. Questions might include what aroused his interest in music or what he thought was his greatest accomplishment.

Students should be able to support their responses.

Use after reading Unit 6, Lesson 2, pages 354–358.

Reading About Folk Heroes

Understand What You Read

DIRECTIONS: In your textbook, you learned about John Henry and Paul Bunyan. Read about a real man who became a folk hero. Then answer the questions that follow.

Johnny Appleseed

John Chapman (1774–1845) was born in Massachusetts. He started his first apple tree nursery in Pennsylvania about 1796. Around 1800 John Chapman started collecting apple seeds and began a long journey planting apple seeds in Ohio, Indiana, and Illinois. He sold or gave away apple seeds to pioneers and some of our apple orchards today are the result of his hard work. John Chapman came to be called "Johnny Appleseed," and the story of his life became a legend. Even though John Chapman was a real man, amazing things have been added to his story to make it larger than life. In one legend Johnny Appleseed began planting seeds after he had a dream of a world filled with apple trees. In other legends Johnny Appleseed is super strong like John Henry or Paul Bunyan. The legend grew as the story of John Chapman's life was told to more and more people.

1. Around 1800 where did John Chapman plant apple seeds?

Ohio, Indiana, and Illinois

2. What was one of the legends told about Johnny Appleseed?

Student answers will vary; they may mention he was super strong or that he began planting seeds after a dream.

3. Why do you think people made John Chapman into a folk hero called Johnny Appleseed?

Student answers will vary. Some students may mention that people wanted to keep the story of John Chapman alive.

HOW TO UNDERSTAND POINT OF VIEW

Pablo Picasso drew many portraits of his son Paulo. Not all the portraits became finished paintings. Sometimes he painted Paulo's picture with toys or animals. Sometimes he painted Paulo in different costumes. The unfinished painting at the right shows Paulo in a clown's costume.

Apply Critical Thinking Skills

DIRECTIONS: Look at the painting at the right. Then answer the questions.

1. How old do you think the boy in the painting is? Answers will vary but will

probably indicate the child is three or four years old.

2. Why do you think the artist shows the little boy dressed as a clown?

Answers might include that clowns are funny and that they are associated with circuses and

good times.

3. Do you think you would like the boy in the painting? Why or why not?

Responses will vary, but answers might include references to the child's sweet expression, to his

calm pose, and to his clown costume.

4. Think about the little boy in the painting and the costume he is wearing. How do you think the painter feels about the boy?

Responses might include that the painter thinks that the boy likes to have fun because of the

costume. The boy's expression, however, is quite serious. A few students might recognize that the

artist knows that there is a serious side to this relationship, too.

HAPPY NEW YEAR
AROUND THE WORLD

People in many lands welcome each new year with a celebration. The celebrations are not the same. People have many customs for New Year's Day activities.

Read for Understanding

DIRECTIONS: Read about some New Year's customs below. Then draw a line from the group to the custom that matches that group.

The first day of the calendar year is a holiday almost everywhere. In the United States, New Year's Day is January 1. Some people celebrate on a different day named by their religion. The Jewish New Year, called *Rosh Hashanah* (RAWSH huh•SHAH•nuh), is in September or early October. Hindus and Muslims celebrate New Year's Day on different days from year to year. The Chinese New Year begins between January 21 and February 19.

To celebrate the new year, people follow customs. For example, many people in the United States make resolutions. Resolutions are promises to act a certain way. In Belgium, children write messages on decorated paper for their families. In China, some people dress up like dragons at the end of a four-day celebration. People of many lands have religious services on New Year's Day.

Group	Custom
Jewish people	Dress up like dragons
People in the United States	Celebrate *Rosh Hashanah*
Children in Belgium	Make resolutions
Chinese people	Write messages to family members

DIRECTIONS: Now it is your turn! Imagine that you are a child in Belgium. On a separate sheet of paper, write a New Year's message to your family. Decorate your message with crayons, markers, or paints.

Use after reading Unit 6, Lesson 4, pages 368–373.

HOW TO FOLLOW a Sequence

Apply Critical Thinking Skills

DIRECTIONS: Below are five statements that have something to do with a Thanksgiving celebration. On the lines at the bottom, write these statements in a paragraph in the proper sequence by connecting the statements with words such as first, then, next, and last.

1. We need Dad's help to carry everything in from the car.

2. The family gathers together on Thanksgiving Day, and we all enjoy the meal!

3. I help Mom and Nana do the shopping.

4. Mom, Dad, Nana, and I cook the meal.

5. We plan our menu—turkey, gravy, stuffing, yams, corn, and my favorite, pecan pie for dessert!

First, we plan our menu—turkey, gravy, stuffing, yams, corn, and my favorite, pecan pie for dessert!

Then, I help Mom and Nana do the shopping. After shopping, we need Dad's help to carry

everything in from the car. Next, Mom, Dad, Nana, and I cook the meal. Finally, the family gathers

together on Thanksgiving Day, and we all enjoy the meal!

The time-order words above are examples only. Students may choose other appropriate time-order

words. Accept reasonable responses.

INDIA

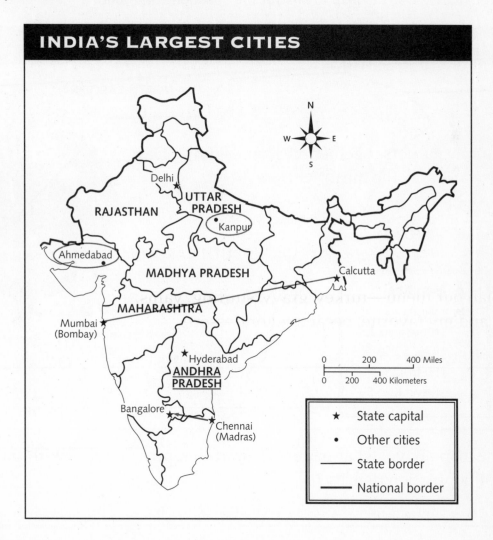

Read a Map

DIRECTIONS: *More than 900 million people live in India. Many of these people live in cities. The map below shows India's largest cities. Study the map. Then complete the activities that follow.*

1. Circle the two cities on the map that are not state capitals.

2. Draw a line that connects the state capital of Maharashtra with Calcutta.

3. Draw an arrow from Chennai to the state capital located to the west.

4. Underline the name of the state of which Hyderabad is the capital.

NAME _____ DATE _____

HOW TO USE A POPULATION MAP

Apply Map and Globe Skills

DIRECTIONS: Use the map to answer the questions that follow.

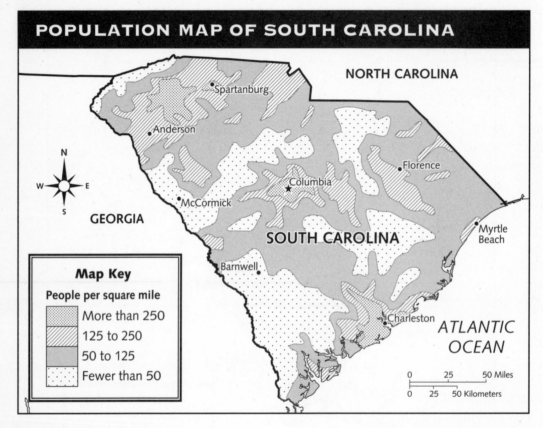

POPULATION MAP OF SOUTH CAROLINA

NORTH CAROLINA

•Spartanburg

•Anderson

•Florence

★Columbia

•McCormick

GEORGIA

SOUTH CAROLINA

Myrtle
Beach

Barnwell•

•Charleston

ATLANTIC
OCEAN

Map Key

People per square mile

More than 250
125 to 250
50 to 125
Fewer than 50

0   25   50 Miles
0   25   50 Kilometers

---

1. On the map above, what pattern is used to represent areas with the largest population density?

the smallest dotted pattern

2. Name three cities with a population density of 125 to 250 people per square mile.

Anderson, Florence, and Myrtle Beach

3. Where is the population least dense? Why do you think that might be?

along the southwestern border; resources are harder to reach.

Use after reading Unit 6, Skill Lesson, pages 384–385.

THE MANY PEOPLE
OF A COMMUNITY

Connect Main Ideas

DIRECTIONS: Use this organizer to show that you understand how the unit's main ideas are connected. Complete this graphic organizer by writing the main idea of each lesson.

Lesson 1
People move from one community to another and from one country to another.

1. People move to follow their _____ religious beliefs.

2. People move to find new _____ opportunities.

Lesson 2
Large communities often have groups of people who share a culture.

1. _____ African Americans move from _____ the South to the North.

2. _____ In the 1920s and 1930s, _____ Harlem became known for _____ its literature, art, and music.

The Many People of a Community

Lesson 4
People of many cultures can live together in one country, community, or neighborhood.

1. Each group may have its _____ own language. Folktales and

2. tall tales can teach lessons or _____ give information about a _____ group's culture.

Lesson 3
Language, customs, food, literature, art, and music are important parts of a culture.

1. People celebrate the New _____ Year in many ways.

2. Special foods and clothing _____ are part of the New Year's _____ celebrations.

Land Features
of the United States

Use a Map

DIRECTIONS: Look at the map of the United States in your textbook on pages A12–A13. List the six types of land features shown in the key on the left side of the map.

1. tundra _____

2. evergreen forest _____

3. mixed forest _____

4. grassland _____

5. arid _____

6. mountain _____

Find Florida on the map, and tell what kind of land you would see there.

mixed forest and grassland
_____

Find the states that border your state. List them below. If your state is bordered by an ocean, list the ocean also.

Answers will vary depending upon students' location. Make sure students have answered the question correctly.
_____

CALIFORNIA'S OTHER GOLD

Read for Understanding

DIRECTIONS: Read the story below and answer the questions.

Water is a resource so important to California that some people call it California's "other type of gold." As California's population grows, more and more people will need this resource. Citizens, farmers, and parks managers all know that people must work together to make sure there is enough water for the future. However, it will not be easy to meet everyone's needs for water. Some people think their needs are more important than the needs of others. What can the citizens of California do? They can work together. Different organizations have already taken steps to find better ways to store the water they have. They have also tried to help teach people how they can conserve, or use less water. Making sure there will be enough water for the future means that all citizens must keep working together to find ways to make sure the "liquid gold" does not run out.

1. Why is water an important resource?

Answers may vary but could include the following: Water is needed for drinking, cooking, farming, swimming, and boating. Accept all reasonable answers.

2. What steps have different organizations already taken?

Some organizations have found better ways to store the water and have helped teach people how to conserve water.

3. Why do the people of California need to work together?

Answers may vary but could include the following: The people of California need to work together because one person alone cannot solve the water problem. Accept all reasonable answers.

USING A
NEIGHBORHOOD MAP

Interpret a Map

DIRECTIONS: *Imagine that the map below represents your neighborhood. Use the compass rose on the map below to help you answer the questions.*

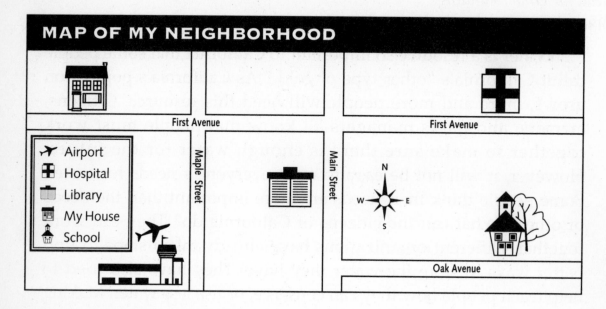

1. How would you get from your home to the school?

go east on First Avenue, next go south on Main Street, and then go east on Oak Avenue

2. If you were at the library and wanted to visit a friend in the hospital, how would you get there?

go north on Main Street and then go east on First Avenue

3. Suppose you were going from your home to the airport to pick up a visiting relative. What route would you follow?

go east on First Avenue and then go south on Maple Street

Use with Write-On Chart 3.

A CITY BY THE BAY

Solve a Word Puzzle

DIRECTIONS: San Francisco is one of the largest cities in California. Read about the history of this community. Then unscramble the words below to form some of the words in this paragraph. The first word has been done for you.

In 1769 Spanish explorers discovered the land around San Francisco. They named it for St. Francis. This land was claimed by the Spanish. The first town, Yerba Buena, was named for mint herbs used for making healing tea. Captain John C. Fremont named the entrance to the bay the Golden Gate because of the yellow and orange poppies that grew on the cliffs. When gold was discovered in 1848 northeast of San Francisco, the town grew very quickly. When silver was discovered, the city grew even more. In 1906 a huge earthquake, followed by fires, destroyed thousands of buildings. The city was rebuilt.

SCRAMBLED WORD	UNSCRAMBLED WORD
rospexelr	explorers
rebsh	herbs
lgdo	gold
virlse	silver
yab	bay
riefs	fires

USING A NATURAL REGIONS MAP

Interpret a Map

DIRECTIONS: Study this map of the natural regions of California. Use the map to answer the questions.

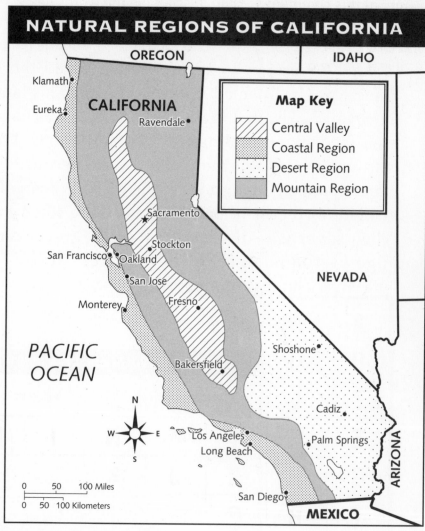

NATURAL REGIONS OF CALIFORNIA

OREGON
IDAHO

Klamath

CALIFORNIA

Eureka

Ravendale

Map Key

Central Valley
Coastal Region
Desert Region
Mountain Region

Sacramento

Stockton

San Francisco   Oakland

San Jose

NEVADA

Monterey   Fresno

Shoshone

PACIFIC OCEAN

Bakersfield

Cadiz

N
W   E
S

Los Angeles
Long Beach

Palm Springs

ARIZONA

0   50   100 Miles
0   50   100 Kilometers

San Diego

MEXICO

1. In what region is Palm Springs located?

Desert Region

2. In what region is the state capital located?

Central Valley

3. Which two regions reach from the north border to the south border of California?

Mountain Region and Coastal Region

Use with Write-On Chart 5.

A RESOURCES
Word Puzzle

Solve a Word Puzzle

DIRECTIONS: Use the words in the box below to find the terms about natural resources in the puzzle. Then circle the words in the puzzle. Words may go down or across. One word has already been circled for you.

tree	mineral
water	air
animal	crop
soil	fuel

A	W	A	T	E	R	E	L	F
O	U	T	U	V	W	X	Y	U
Z	L	A	M	N	O	P	E	E
E	F	I	A	N	I	M	A	L
G	H	R	J	K	L	I	R	S
T	R	P	U	V	W	N	O	I
A	E	I	T	R	E	E	B	C
D	F	H	G	I	L	R	J	K
V	U	W	C	D	E	A	T	W
J	K	L	R	P	O	L	X	A
A	D	S	O	I	L	F	E	D
B	E	C	P	Z	Q	T	R	I

COMMUNITIES
Can Change

Complete a Word Puzzle

DIRECTIONS: Use the clues below to fill in the puzzle with the ideas you have learned about communities and change. After you finish, read the letters inside the boxes from top to bottom. These letters will make a word that you can use to answer the question.

Clues

1. A place where people live and work is a ___.

2. When everyone leaves an area after fast change, that place is called a ___.

3. A ___ causes great harm to a place.

4. ___ helps a place grow in an organized way.

5. A town is ___ when people move there and businesses are built there.

6. When the population stops growing and businesses close, an area is in a ___.

1. c o m m u n i t y

2. g h o s t   t o w n

3. d i s a s t e r

4. p l a n n i n g

5. g r o w i n g

6. d e c l i n e

What happens to communities both suddenly and over time? __change_____

Which Choice Is Best?

Use Critical Thinking Skills

DIRECTIONS: Each pair of pictures below shows a choice you might make to help prevent pollution. Circle the one that is best for the Earth. Color the picture you circled.

1. On Saturday a group of your friends is meeting at a neighborhood park to play baseball. How will you get there?

2. You are in charge of cleaning up after a family camping trip. Where will you put the trash?

3. You would like more books and toys. Which place will you shop?

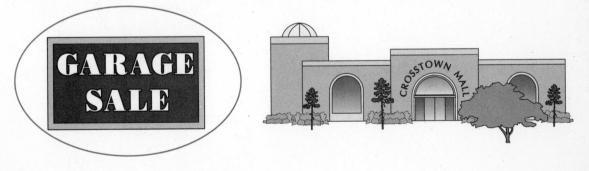

GARAGE SALE

CROSSTOWN MALL

From
Sheep to Sweater

Identify a Process

DIRECTIONS: The pictures below show four steps in making a product. Draw a line between each picture and the correct step.

1. Get the raw materials.

2. Spin the wool into yarn.

3. Make the yarn into a sweater.

4. Sell the finished product.

Use with Write-On Chart 9.

MAKING
CONSUMER CHOICES

Apply Critical Thinking Skills

DIRECTIONS: Imagine you earned a total of $20.00 from doing chores for your family and for neighbors. From the items below, decide which ones you will buy. Circle the pictures of the items you choose. On the lines below, explain why you made these choices.

$3.00 $5.00 $1.00

$20.00 $10.00

$2.00 $15.00 $4.00

I made the choice I did because

Students' responses will vary, but the cost of the choices added up should not exceed $20.00.

Accept all reasonable explanations.

WORKING TOGETHER
TO SOLVE A PROBLEM

Put Events in Sequence

DIRECTIONS: A beach near you is littered. Listed below are several steps you could take to clean up the beach. Number the steps in the order you would follow.

___4___ Then have each volunteer clean up one small area of the beach.

___1___ Talk to people in your neighborhood about the litter problem and ask for volunteers to help you.

___3___ When everyone is at the beach, make sure they have gloves and plastic sacks to collect trash.

___2___ Now that volunteers have agreed to help you, tell them when cleanup will be and where to meet.

___5___ After the clean up, call the newspaper office and tell them what your volunteer group has done to clean up the beach.

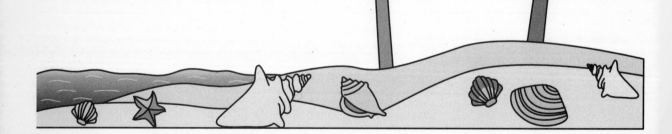

THE CALIFORNIA FLAG

Understand What You Have Read

DIRECTIONS: Read the story about the California flag and answer the questions that follow.

CALIFORNIA REPUBLIC

In the 1840s California belonged to Mexico. Some of the people living on the land were unhappy about the laws and wanted them changed. They also wanted to be free from Mexican rule. Captain John C. Fremont came to California in 1846 and helped the men who wanted to break away from Mexico. On June 14, 1846, the men captured Fort Sonoma and raised the Bear Flag. The flag was homemade, with a single star, a red stripe, a grizzly bear, and the words "California Republic." The star meant that California was an independent republic. The bear was a warning to Mexico that the men would fight for their freedom, which they did. This flag was adopted as the official California state flag in 1911.

1. Why did the settlers in California become upset with Mexico? because they were unhappy with the laws and wanted them to change

2. What did the star on the Bear Flag stand for? It meant that California was an independent republic.

3. What did the bear stand for? The bear was a warning that the settlers would fight for freedom.

4. When did California adopt this flag as the state flag? 1911

Use with Write-On Chart 12.

You Are the *Artist*

Draw and Explain a Picture

DIRECTIONS: You have learned that different things are important to different painters. Some painters like to paint people while others like to paint animals or birds. Some painters use bright colors, while others use dull colors. Now it is your turn to draw something that is important to you. Put your drawing in the frame below. You may use colored pencils, pens, or markers. Underneath your picture write a sentence that explains your drawing.

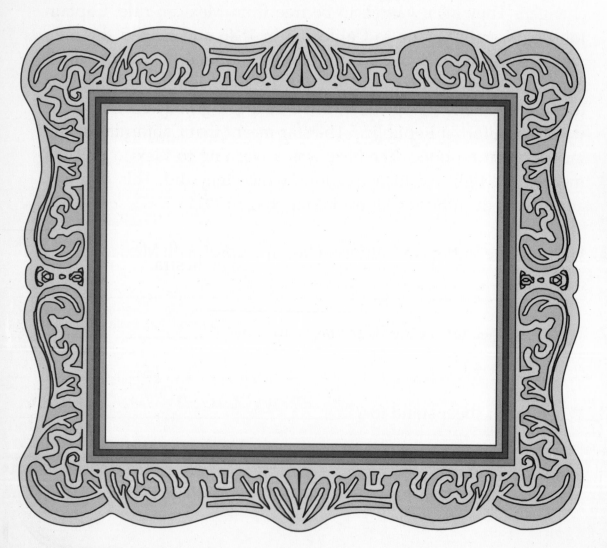

Students' sentences will vary, but should adequately explain the drawings.

_____

_____

Use with Write-On Chart 13.

Understanding Percussion Instruments

Understand What You Have Read

DIRECTIONS: Read the paragraph below, then answer each of the questions about musical instruments.

You have looked at some of the kinds of drums used around the world. Drums are part of the group of instruments called *percussion instruments*. The word *percussion* means that sound is made when the instrument is shaken or hit, either with a stick or the hands. When people play their instruments together in an orchestra, percussion instruments are only one group. Other instruments are part of string, woodwind, or brass groups. The percussion instruments are usually in the back of the orchestra. Pictured below are some common percussion instruments.

1. Drums are part of the group of instruments called _percussion_____.

2. To make a sound on a percussion instrument, you would _hit or shake it_____.

3. Name one other group of instruments in an orchestra.

Students may select string, woodwind, or brass.
_____

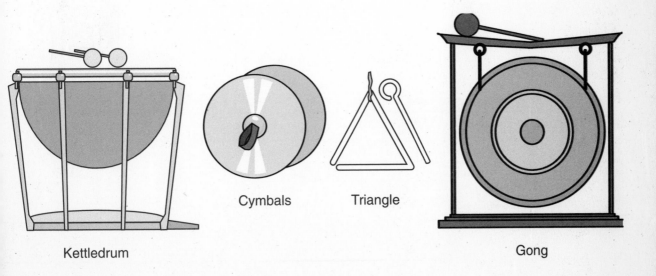

Kettledrum   Cymbals   Triangle   Gong